INNOVATING FOR RURAL MARKETS IN INDIA

Dr. SUBHO CHATTOPADHYAY

MBA, PhD.

Associate Professor

LBSIMT, Bareilly

DEDICATED TO MY PARENTS

Dr. SHYAMAL KUMAR CHATTOPADHYAY

&

Mrs. RANU CHATTOPADHYAY

A TRIBUTE & OBEISANCE
TO
HIS HOLINESS SHRI MUKTESWAR MAHARAJ
JEE

CONTENT

PREFACE

*Inventions enrich our lives; innovations simplify them;
Inventions open up the path to development; innovations
lead us on to such path.*

The Meaning of Innovation:

Finding out something that nobody ever knew is invention. Adding

value to the invention and putting it to a productive use profitably is

innovation. Thus, while Benjamin Franklin discovered electricity,

Thomas Alva Edison put this discovery into a novel use and

invented the electric bulb, a product that offered an immense value

proposition and carried a tremendous business potential. Such value

laden invention transformed this greatest of inventors to the league

of the greatest innovators of the planet. Though innovations may

span a number of functional areas and a spectrum of activities, they

can broadly be classified into two categories: *Radical innovations*

and *incremental innovations*. Thus when Henry Ford juggled with

the idea of a motor engine replacing the horses in a horse drawn

carriage and conjured up an image of a motor driven carriage, it was

a radical innovation. The innovation not only brought a radical change in the way people travelled from one place to another but also opened up an array of business possibilities. This radical innovation propelled the genesis and growth of a new industry and an array of supporting industries.

Types of Innovations:

Though radical innovation may seem to hold the promise of a big change, it may not always be the most suitable type of innovation. Organizations that decide to use innovation as an instrument of growth and as a strategic tool may have at their disposal at least eight forms of innovation which include customer centric innovation, outcome driven innovation, disruptive innovation, management innovation, open innovation, value innovation, architectural innovation and radical innovation.

Customer centric innovation refers to an innovation that has concern for the customer at its epicenter. The innovator's main objective is to solve a problem for the customer. The pre requisite for this type of innovation is empathy for the customer.

A form of customer centric innovation is the 'outcome driven innovation'. Outcome driven innovation focuses on the final oucome sought be the consumer from an activity. It undertakes to enhance the outcome derived by the consumer from the company's products and services and links the value creation activities of the company to customer defined metrics.

Disruptive innovations are innovations that disrupt the existing market and technology, replace the old technology with new technology and create new markets and segments that have never been thought of.

In contrast to the commonly discussed business innovations which involve innovations in the forms and designs of products, management innovations consist of innovative ways of managing and include innovations in the process of planning, organizing, leading, coordinating and motivating.

Open innovation is an innovation initiated and done by any individual, group or company from anywhere around the world, tapped by the organization and adopted by it. It is an innovation that is not formally developed within the organization in question.

Value innovation is one that brings about a significant change in the value proposition offered by the company. It is commensurate with a radically different technology and product.

A significant and radical change in the value delivery process creates architectural innovation.

Radical innovation is a discontinuous leap in the present technology as well as in the present process of doing the job.

Each type of innovation has its own benefits, advantages and use. The type of innovation an organization would involve in would depend on the structure of the organization, its financial strength, business philosophy and the markets it is targeting.

Prerequisite for Innovation: An Environment Conducive for Innovation & Innovation Oriented Culture:

Notwithstanding the type of innovation that would be most suitable for an organization, an essential prerequisite for embarking on the route of regular innovation is the environment that favours innovation. Such a suitable environment in turn has to be created by developing a culture that infuses the propensity to innovate and kindles the desire to tread on the path of innovation. It simply implies that the most important factor that makes the organizational environment conducive for innovation is the culture of the organization carefully crafted to nurture innovation. Innovative organizations are often found to have reared an ecosystem conducive to innovation by imbibing the values of innovation into the work culture and by inculcating the same values into the employees of the organization. The culture of innovation is thus built into the DNA of the organization. One of the most important roles of an organizational leader in such a case is to foster the culture of innovation, nurture the innovation friendly ecosystem and preserve the DNA of the organization that would breed continuous innovation and ensure a sustainable growth for the organization.

Innovations are often associated with risk and many organizations, intimated by the possibility of an immediate failure from innovation and by an overestimation of the probabilities of a failed innovation, perceive innovation as a threat or a risk factor. Irony lies in the fact that an organization that shies away from innovation races ahead towards its stagnation and consequent demise. An ability to take such a risk therefore ensures sustainability and survival. So, it goes without saying that innovation is a function of the environment of the organization, its culture and its ability to take risk.

A fact established beyond doubt is that the culture of innovation in an organization is contingent on the dynamism of its leadership, its propensity to take risk, its attitude towards experimentation and the direction provided by it. Business leaders who understand, appreciate and propagate the concept that risk is a part of doing business are able to accelerate the pace of innovation driven growth and catapult the organization to a higher pedestal.

The book dwells upon the essentiality of innovation for developing the Indian rural market and advocates using simple and suitable innovation for penetrating the rural market of India. The Indian rural market is a market that is continually evolving and is rapidly catching up with the urban market. This is a market which despite its fast paced evolution is remarkably different from the urban market.

The marketers aspiring to reign over the rural markets are faced with issues and challenges very different from the challenges they had faced in the conventional urban markets they are generally familiar with.

The strategies, products, sales formats and value propositions offered by them in their urban markets are either partially workable or completely unworkable in the rural settings. The rural markets at times call for an entire new set of offerings from the companies. This mandates innovation for successfully operating and surviving in the rural markets. It would do well for a player operating in the Indian rural market to think of rural India as a producer and as a consumer and thereafter categorise the challenges and problems in two distinct categories: challenges related to rural market as a producer and those related to rural market as a consumer. Innovations directed at the rural market too need to be worked upon, conceptualized and executed as innovations that empower the rural producers and innovations that empower the rural consumers.

****

CHAPTER 1

THE INDIAN RURAL MARKET, RURAL CONSUMER & THE SCOPE OF INNOVATION: A PRELUDE

While thinking of rural India as producers and endeavouring to figure out innovations that would empower the rural producers and solve their problems, it is important to consider certain facts. India has predominately being an agrarian economy where approximately 60% of the population is directly or indirectly dependent on agriculture. According to the official website of the Indian government, agriculture provides the principal means of livelihood for over 58.4% of India's population (Refer: http://www.archive.india.gov.in/sectors/agriculture/index.php).

Despite this fact agriculture contribute to nearly 18% of the nation's GDP. This provides ample evidence of the stark negligence of the agricultural sector and it clearly demonstrates the apathy of the policy makers and the implementation machinery towards the development of rural India. Dwindling of opportunities in the agricultural sector because of lack of initiative by the government machinery has forced many a rural folk to migrate to urban areas in search of livelihood, jobs and opportunities. It is further estimated by NCAER that 45% of the country's population will be residing in cities and towns by 2050 up from 30% now. This urban influx over a period of time has siphoned the productive human capital and priceless human resource from the villages and put a tremendous burden on the urban resources. The consequent population imbalance and non exploitation of the pool of natural resources in the rural areas further act as a drag on the national economic development and inhibit the social development. According to the NCAER report 2010, India's top 20 cities account for just 10% of the country's population but earn 31% of its income, spend 21% and are responsible for more that 65% of surplus income. In sharp contrast to 67% of the country's surplus income being earned by the urban population, the rural population accounts for only a third. In the prevalent situation, strengthening of the rural infrastructural facilities aimed at increasing the rural productivity, connecting the rural producers to the urban markets and the rural consumers to the urban producers, availability of training and education facilities for the rural masses, up gradation of the technological, attitudinal and social skills of the rural folk and the development of health care facilities in the villages are not merely desirable steps but have become the utmost priority and essential prerequisite to stop the influx and to continue on the highway of economic development. This gives an inkling of the priority areas on which focus has to be there for systematic, planned innovation. Three such priority areas are infrastructure, education and training and healthcare.

The rural market till long had been thought of as an inaccessible, unsubstantial market with limited purchasing power. This belief has prompted the marketers to blatantly evade the call of the rural markets. The truth of the matter is that all rural consumers are not poor. As revealed by the study conducted by NCAER, 'there are as many middle income and above households in the rural areas as there are in the urban areas'. The catch is that a sizeable portion of the rural consumer does not prefer to buy in bulk but have a propensity to buy in small amounts as and when required. This presses on the need for some change in the products, services and packaging and opens up a strong case in favour of innovation for the rural markets. Moreover the scattered and fragmented nature of the Indian rural markets makes distribution a cumbersome process.

Unlike that in the urban areas, a member of the distribution channel in the rural area would end up catering to significantly lesser number of consumers in an area of comparable size. Establishing an intensively wide and deep distribution channel may not always be economically viable and profitable. This presents another scope for innovation for the marketer intending to penetrate into the rural markets. Other pertinent questions which may be answered through innovation are: how to sell profitably to the rural poor, how to reduce the cost of marketing communication and yet communicate more effectively with the rural masses, how to deliver an enhanced value to the consumers, what type of business models to develop for the rural markets, how to lower the price of the products and services for the rural consumers, how to make the products more cost effective and many more.

The book attempts to give a brief account of the Indian rural market, explore the possibility of using innovation for penetrating into this market and point to and justify the suitability of some specific types of innovations for the rural market of India.

****

CHAPTER 2

RURAL MARKET IN INDIA

Many years ago the Father of the Nation, Mahatma Gandhi, had said that India lives in its villages. India lives in its villages even today. According to the 2011 Census of India, 68.84 percent of the population resides in villages. India was and continues to be an agrarian economy. 60.5 percent of the land is under agricultural cultivation (Source: http://data.worldbank.org). Moving out of the thickly populated Indian cities and towns, one finds vast stretches of agricultural land. Surrounding these agricultural fields are the villages inhabited by the vast majority of Indians. This is where the soul of the country resides. This is where one experiences the palpable existence of the great Indian civilization and can expect to discover the true essence of the country- India. These villages along with their people, their markets and adjoining agricultural plot comprise rural India. However for the sake of operational convenience, the term rural has been defined in different ways by different organizations.

The census of India 2011, defines rural as all those areas which are not urban. According to the 2011 census, urban area refers to the following:

a) All places with a municipality, corporation or cantonment or notified town area

b) All places which satisfy the following criteria

    i.   Minimum population of 5000

    ii.   At least 75 percent of the male working population is non agricultural

    iii.   A density of population of at least 400 per square Km (ie, 1000 per square mile)

The above definition of an urban area implies that a rural area may refer to:

a) All places which do not have a municipality, corporation or cantonment

b) All places which satisfy the following criteria:

    i.   Population of less than 5000

    ii.   More than 25 percent of the male working population engaged in agriculture

iii.   A density of population of less than 400 per square Km.

According to India's central bank, The Reserve Bank of India, a place may be classified as a rural area if its population is less than 10,000. The Planning Commission of India considers villages and towns up to a population of 15,000 as rural. The National Bank for Agriculture and Rural Development (NABARD) refers to all villages and towns with population of less than 50,000 as rural areas.

Some companies operating in the Indian market like LG Electronics go to the extreme of considering all places other than the seven metros in the country as rural.

Such disparity in definition may make it difficult to comprehend the meaning of 'Rural' in India. Notwithstanding the risk of oversimplification, a rural area may be thought of as a place beyond cities where the major occupation of the residents is agriculture. Small towns with modest standard of living with or without agriculture being the major occupation may also be considered rural.

CHARACTERISTICS OF THE INDIAN RURAL MARKET

> Being majorly dependant on Agriculture, the income of a significant percentage of the rural people is seasonal.

> Because of seasonal income, the rural market experiences spurts in consumption during harvest seasons.

> Disposable income of a huge chunk of the market is less. Thus a majority of the rural consumers refrain from buying in bulk and prefer to buy in small lots.

> A serious problem faced by the rural people is that of unemployment, disguised employment and low income.

> Because of the revolution in information and communication technology and because of mobile phone penetration, the rural folks are well aware of the changes taking place in the world. Brand awareness is also strong.

> Low standard of living in many areas.

> The rural people spend a major part of their income on necessity items and daily need items (Source: Shanthi

Kannan, "Rural Market- A World of Opportunity", The Hindu, October 11, 2001).

➢ Literacy rate in rural areas is lesser as compared to that in urban areas (68.9% in rural areas as against 84.9% in urban areas) (Source: Census, 2013) but has improved over the years.

➢ Joint Family system is prevalent.

➢ Reference groups have strong influence on consumers.

Physical Characteristics of Rural Markets

➢ Modern amenities are missing in many rural areas.

➢ Infrastructure (Roads, Transportation, Availability of Drinking Water, Electricity, etc.) is significantly poor.

➢ For some villages situated in remote areas, accessibility to markets is difficult.

➢ Health and Education are areas of concern. Medical facilities and education facilities are not suitably developed in most of the rural areas.

PROBLEMS AND PROSPECTS IN THE INDIAN RURAL MARKET

Despite more than 70 percent of the Indian population residing in villages, the Indian rural market has not been tapped properly by the marketers till this day. It is only now that the companies have started exploring the rural market, though not to the hilt. One of the reasons for the Indian and foreign companies to have abstained from engaging with the rural markets of India is the widely scattered and fragmented nature of the rural markets.

There are a good number of villages that are so remotely located that the marketer does not find it feasible to lay down a full-fledged distribution network and commence sales operations in these areas. For villagers in these areas life is difficult as they do not have an easy access to the market. For many such village folks, even things of day to day need are not available in their vicinity. There are places where people have to travel 25 to 50 km before they can reach their nearest market. For villages surrounded by forests, things are even more difficult.

Absence of pukka/metallic roads and badly maintained roads make things worse. Even companies and marketers willing to reach out to these areas do not dare to take the initiative owing to the poor infrastructure in these places. Bad roads, unavailability of transportation facilities, irregular supply or no supply of electricity and unavailability of good quality potable water keeps these marketers away from these untapped, remote villages.

Even in some rural areas that are well connected to the cities, the gifts of modern technology have eluded the lives of the people there. People are bereft of the modern amenities that make life easy and fast. They continue to remain in deprivation of proper medical facilities and education facilities. Health and education for these places are the areas of concern and focus for the Government of India. Many government schemes and policies have been formulated and are being implemented for the improvement of health and education of the rural masses.

The Indian rural market had for long been thought of as a market with limited potential. The rural consumer was thought of as a poor consumer who is neither willing nor able to spend substantially on consumption. This notion/ perception of an average marketer has however been proved wrong in the last two decades. Introduction of products (particularly FMCG products) in sachets, small packs and value packs have revolutionized the rural marketing concept and have brought in an unprecedented dynamism into the seemingly sleepy and dormant rural market. The introduction of products in small packs by companies like Cavinkare and the launch of simple formulations products in ultra simple packs and modest price by companies like Nirma and Parle have made them the pioneers of rural marketing. Similarly, a tweak in the business model, product offerings in particular, of some hitherto urban marketing companies like Hindustan Unilever and ITC have made them the champions of the rural market.

Pattern of Income Governs Rural Consumption/ Determines the Nature of Rural Consumption

Much of the false notion of the companies regarding the lackadaisical attitude of the rural people towards consumption can be attributed to the typical purchase behavior and spending habits of the Indian rural consumers. Around 58 percent of the rural population is dependent on agriculture (Source: NSSO Report on "Key Indicators of Situation of Agricultural Households in India", Jan-Dec, 2013).

These agriculturists have a seasonal income. The harvest seasons bring money to them. Thus during the harvest seasons a spurt in spending and consumption can be witnessed in the rural markets. After relative extravagance in spending during these seasons, the left over income is saved to be spent throughout the year. This gives rise to the psychological compulsion to be cautious in spending for the remaining part of the year. This psychological compulsion makes the rural folk apparently parsimonious in his consumption and spending. Thus, instead of buying in bulk, he prefers to buy in small lots and small quantities which gives him the satisfaction of spending less in each purchase or transaction. The purchase quantity at times may be so small so as to last a single use or two uses.

A certain percentage (more than 33 percent) of the rural people consists of daily wage earners and agricultural labourers (Source: Gurpreet Wasi, "Small Town and Rural India- The Dawn of New Consumption, Economic Times, April 23, 2015). According to the Centre for Global Development report published in November, 2012, 33.8 percent of rural people fall into the category of low income group. These people have low disposable income. Even for these people buying FMCG goods that would last a number of uses does not make any sense. They find buying in bulk packages monetarily and psychologically impractical and prefer to buy in small quantities and small packages instead.

This segment of consumer is highly price sensitive. This however does not imply that the consumers who constitute this segment would settle for inferior goods. They are value conscious at the same time and aggressively seek value for their money. The revolution in the information and communication technology has made them much aware of the various brands available in the market. This new breed of brand conscious rural consumers assess the brand and opts for those brands that offer the best value proposition at a reasonable price and preferably in small packs. It would be a gross mistake to think of the entire Indian rural market as consisting of these very consumers. According to the Centre for Global Development report, 2012, if the middle income range is considered to be $8-$50 per capita per day, 48.33 million people fall in the middle income group in the rural areas in contrast to 42.80 million people in the urban areas (Source: Christian Meyer, Nancy Birdsall, "New Estimates of India's Middle Class - Technical Note", Center for Global Development, November, 2012). An old NCAER report also suggested that "at the highest income level there are 2.3 million urban households as against 1.6 million households in rural areas." (Source: Shanthi Kannan, "Rural Market- A World of Opportunity", The Hindu, October 11, 2001). The norms of consumption for these consumers may not match those of a typical rural consumer or a typical urban consumer. Their consumption behavior, in turn, would be a varying mix of the behavior of the two categories of consumers. Such diversity in the rural markets makes the rural markets a bit confusing and does not permit formulation of a standard set of norms for rural marketing. Despite these constraints and limitations, the rural markets constitute a major chunk of the country's population. A population of 85.7 Crores (Source: http://data.worldbank.org/indicator/SP.RUR.TOTL) translates to 12.24 percent of the global population (As per the press release of United Nations Information Centre for India and Bhutan on July 10, 2014, the population of rural India is 857 million [Source: http://www.unic.org.in/display.php?E=13443&K=Population] and as per the United nations, the global population has crossed 7 billion [Source: "Concise Report on the World Population Situation in 2014", Department of Economic and Social Affairs- Population

Division,United Nations, New York, 2014]). Such juggernaut of a market cannot be and should not be left unattended and un-catered. It is a potential market much greater in size than the urban market. A section of the bottom of the pyramid lies in this rural market. In this rural market consumers are there, needs are there and scope of consumption is there but the ways of consumption and the trends of consumption are different from those of the urban markets. Consumers are willing to buy and spend but not perhaps in the same way their urban counterparts do. The value proposition sought by the rural consumers may be significantly different from those sought by the urban consumers. This fact drives in the necessity of thoughtful and relevant innovations.

NEED FOR INNOVATION FOR THE INDIAN RURAL MARKET

Wherever there is human life, need for goods and services has to be there. This simple truth justifies the fact that a substantial need for goods and services exist even in the backward, untapped hinterlands and point to the existence of a substantial market scope in the rural areas. While the rural people want goods and services, the manufacturers and marketers are also eager to expand their market and even penetrate into untapped and virgin markets in the process. Conceptually the rural markets provide a mutually beneficial proposition for the urban sellers and the rural buyers. Problem however arises as the marketer, used to selling in the urban markets and the developed markets, is not habitual of selling in the forms and formats suitable for the underprivileged rural consumers. Similarly the rural consumer doesn't find it suitable or convenient or easy to buy in the forms and formats commonly used by these sellers in their conventional markets (read urban markets and developed markets). This gives rise to a marketing gap and a seemingly insurmountable rift is formed between the market and the marketer (ie, between the buyer and the seller).

This gap, this marketing problem calls for unconventional thinking. The need and desire to narrow down this gap urgently calls for a variety of innovation ranging from a simple innovation in product packaging to a more sophisticated innovation in product technology. Innovations may be employed in different domains or spheres to alleviate the market gap. Smooth entry into the rural markets and consolidation there may be facilitated through the use of innovations in:

❖ Product form/ Product formulation

❖ Product Packaging

❖ Manufacturing technique

❖ Mechanism of delivery

❖ Selling format

❖ Supply chain

❖ Distribution

❖ Pricing techniques, etc.

Examples abound of companies and individuals who have innovated in one or more of the above mentioned areas so as to effectively reach out to and cater to the Indian rural market.

****

CHAPTER 3

INNOVATIONS FOR THE RURAL MARKET

Innovations transform the way we think, live and work. Innovations big and small have been known to bring about a significant change in business, economy and lifestyle. Innovations may be classified into various categories and may be related to different things. However, in all business related and business relevant innovations, the two arenas (or two dimensions of innovation) can be identified as business model innovation and technological innovation. A combination of different types of technological innovation and business model innovation give rise to several different categories of innovation.

Contrary to commonly held perception, all innovation need not be technology innovation or technology intensive innovation. Much can be achieved and is achieved through altering the business model. Significant and relevant changes in the way of doing business may open up new vistas and possibilities. Business model innovation may help tap new markets and visibly non potential market segments. It may whip up lucrative business opportunities in segments and sectors where none seems to exit. Technology innovation on the other hand may refer to tweaking the technology to enhance the value offered to the customer. It may also mean coming up with an entirely new technology which would create new products or new value proposition for the customer. Thus when Ford introduced a motor drawn carriage into the market, it replaced the horse drawn carriage that was the order of the day showing a new and superior way of solving the same old problem of locomotion and transportation. The company provided a superior value beyond the imagination of the consumer of that era by offering locomotion in speed, style and convenience. The company along with its product, the car, revolutionized the concept of locomotion. The car by the Ford Company thus stood out to differentiate itself from other modes of locomotion by virtue of its ability to offer the basic value proposition (locomotion) along with the enhanced value proposition (represented by speed, style and convenience). The Ford Motor Company made use of an entirely new technology and gave rise to a product that was absolutely new to the world and very different from all other existing products. This type of innovation is referred to as technology innovation. To illustrate the difference between technology innovation and business innovation an example of innovation can be cited from another industry in a different era-The example of Dominos Pizza. In India Dominos differentiates itself from its competitors on the basis of its ability to deliver a freshly prepared Pizza to its customers at the latter's desired location within half an hour from the receipt of the order. The ingredients used in the product or the core product itself might not be exceptionally superior to that of its competitors. The company does not even use any distinctively different technology for making the pizzas. The difference lies in the company's additional expertise in home delivery and its equitable focus on home delivery. The company's willingness and ability to deliver the desired satisfaction at a place chosen by the customer is a simple, inexpensive and 'non radical' innovation which gives the brand 'The Top of Mind Awareness' that every company vies for. This type of innovation that emerges from the modification of the business model and does not involve any alteration in the technology can be referred to as business model innovation.

The specific points of innovation within the area of technology innovation are product and service innovation, process innovation and enabling technologies innovation. The specific points of innovation within the area of business model innovation are value proposition innovation, innovation in value network/supply chain and target customer innovation. These six areas of innovation have been referred to as the six levers of innovation by Davila, et al. in their book Making Innovation Work.

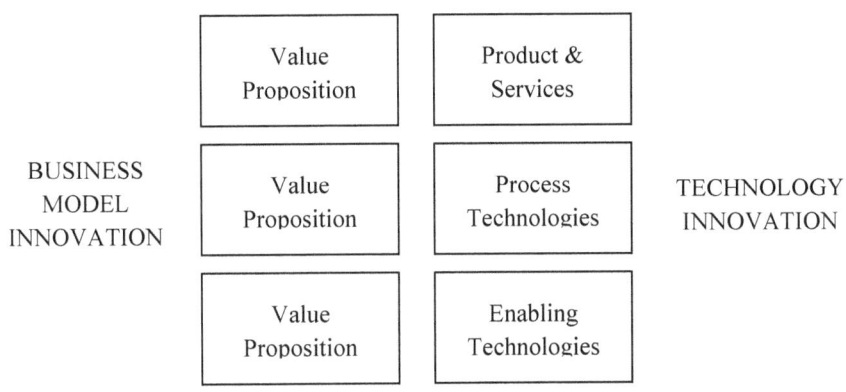

FIGURE 1: THE SIX LEVERS OF INNOVATION
Source: Davila, Tony; Epstein, Marc J. & Shelton Robert; "Making Innovation Work", Pearson Education (New Delhi),

A combination of different degree of Technology innovation and Business Model innovation gives rise to incremental innovation, semi-radical innovation or radical innovation.

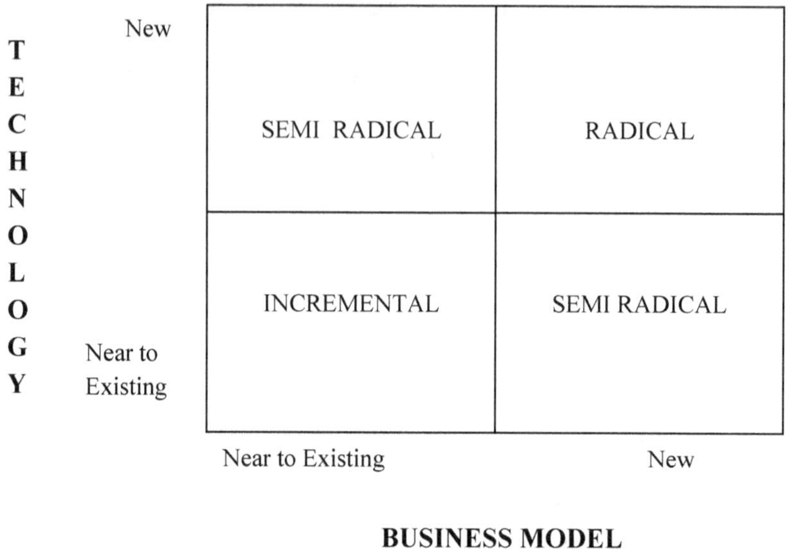

	Near to Existing	New
New (TECHNOLOGY)	SEMI RADICAL	RADICAL
Near to Existing (TECHNOLOGY)	INCREMENTAL	SEMI RADICAL

Near to Existing   New

BUSINESS MODEL

FIGURE 2: THE INNOVATION FRAMEWORK

Source: Davila, Tony; Epstein, Marc J. & Shelton Robert; "Making Innovation Work", Pearson Education (New Delhi). 2008

It can be inferred from the discussion that any minor change in all or some of the six levers of innovation is an incremental innovation. A significant change in any or all of the technology innovation drivers (ie, product and service, process technology and enabling technology) accompanied with some change in all or some of the business model related innovation drivers (ie, value proposition, value network and target customer) qualifies as Technology Driven Semi Radical Innovation.

Business Model Driven Semi Radical Innovation, on the other hand refers to a significant change in business model related innovation drivers and small change in all or some of the technology related innovation drivers.

A major change in both the group of innovation drivers results in Radical Innovation. As radical innovation consists of a major change in technology and business model, it usually involves a lavish investment and elaborate expenditure on Research & Development. Radical innovation is usually the foundation of a Blue Ocean Strategy.

Each of these three innovations, ie, Incremental Innovation, Semi Radical Innovation and Radical Innovation differ from the other in its scope, use, relevance and benefit. An incremental innovation may bring about some noticeable change to the product or business model without incurring a heavy cost. Technology driven Semi Radical innovation may usher in a fresh look to the product, and offer an enhanced experience with the service of the company. When the objective is to overhaul the business without significantly altering the technology of the product or the manufacturing technology,

Business Model driven Semi Radical innovation ideally suits the purpose. Radical innovation is the prerogative of the market driving companies. It involves greater investment, greater risk and exponentially greater rewards if successful. It may give rise to a new product category and may even result in the emergence of new sectors and new markets to compete in. Different situations require the use of different types innovations. The suitability of an innovation for a business varies according to the business environment, the market, extent of competition, technological environment, dynamism of the market, the type of industry, the nature of business and the size and turnover of the organization. Thus for a market leader with a wide geographical coverage, established brand and illustrious business history, radical innovation can be attempted relatively easily. On the other hand for a small player with limited financial resources operating in a small market, the more appropriate type of innovation is the incremental innovation.

While talking of rural markets one can appreciate the fact that rural markets are largely untapped till date and hence offer a wide scope of experimentation. These markets can serve as hotbeds of innovative products, innovative business models and innovative solutions. Because of the wide expanse over which the market is spread, and the huge number of need sets that lie untapped, this market offers scope for large number of innovations in products, services and solutions. However as economy forms an important criteria of purchase for the rural consumer, the scope of innovation becomes somewhat restricted and limited to those types of innovation that do not incur a heavy cost and are able to offer an affordable and low priced solution to the customers. Thus for innovative products which are very costly, the rural market may not be a substantial market and hence is not an appropriate market for hardcore radical innovations.

Notwithstanding this concession, the Indian rural market has been witness to some highly relevant innovation worth mentioning and the market can safely be attributed as a nursery to a new genre of business model innovation and frugal innovation. The rural market has evolved in a big way in the last few decades and continues to evolve further. The evolution can be attributed to a number of big and small innovations over the years. Some innovations worthy of being cited are:

(1) White Revolution in India (Operation Flood): 'Operation Flood', initiated and implemented under the leadership of Verghese Kurien, not only made India self sufficient in milk production but also made the country the largest producer of milk in the world (Source: "Taking Liberties: Poor People, Free Trade and Trade Justice", Ed. Pendleton, Andrew & Narayanan, Pradeep; Christian Aid Publishing; p. 35). The success of Operation Flood can be attributed to an innovative business model. The highlight of the business model lies in the innovation brought about in the supply chain system. Traditionally milk was produced by the marginal farmers (usually possessing a small herd of cattle) who sold the milk to the ultimate consumers or in the mandis (markets) through the middlemen. While the customer paid a high price for the milk, the farmer used to get a very small price for his product. The chunk of the profit would be pocketed by the middleman. Milk being a highly perishable product, was sold only in the nearby markets, and was scarcely available in the non milk producing areas and states.

Operation Flood was instrumental in the formation of a number of cooperative societies across a number of villages in Gujrat and later on in a number of other states in India. The farmers would sell their milk to these cooperatives from where AMUL would collect the milk, process it, package it and distribute it across the country. The 'AMUL' model has now been replicated across the country. Today there are 1,44246 dairy cooperative societies in India that collect milk from 15 million producers. The milk collected by these village milk cooperative societies is then sent to the District Milk Cooperative Unions where the milk is processed. The processed milk and milk products are finally marketed by the state milk federations. There are 177 district cooperative unions across the country and there are 22 state marketing federations that distribute the milk in the various markets across the country (Source: www.amul.com).

It goes without saying that the milk unions use state of the art technology for preserving, processing and packaging milk and milk products. Nonetheless, the credit for the success of the model goes to innovatively designed supply chain system (the system of milk collection). The 'AMUL' model of business can be categorised as Business Model driven Semi Radical innovation.

(2) ITC e-Chaupal: e-Chaupal is another widely cited success story and an apt example of inclusive growth through business model innovation. Initiated by the International Marketing division of ITC and implemented under the leadership of Y.C. Deveshwar, e-Chaupal has done a commendable job in strengthening the supply chain of the FMCG giant while simultaneously empowering the rural agriculturists, enabling them to grow and prosper,

The farmers across India had to avail the services of middlemen to sell their produce in the mandis. The wares often passed though several levels of middlemen before reaching the mandis from where they were purchased by the final consumer. In the process the price at which the final consumer bought was substantially high than the price at which the farmer sold it to the middleman. A major portion of the margin is pocketed by the middleman and the farmer ends up being the biggest loser. Another problem associated with this system is that the market information flows to the farmers through the middlemen in the distribution channel. These middlemen are known to block or allow the flow of information as per their convenience. Unavailability of proper information related to market and farming would make the farmers dependant on the marketing intermediaries.

The e-Chaupal model of ITC intervenes to overhaul the agricultural distribution system by systematising the flow of information to the farmers and curbing the dominance of intermediaries. The word 'Chaupal' refers to the main meeting place in a village. Drawing from this concept, ITC goes on to erect an internet kiosk in each of the villages it targets. The kiosk is furnished with a computer terminal with an internet connection. It would be managed by an elected representative of the farmers called the 'Sanchalak' which means 'Coordinator'. The farmers would access the e-Chaupal to gather information related to the markets, price, weather and agricultural inputs like seeds, fertilizers, etc. E-Chaupal would also connect the farmers to the big and small consumers, thus reducing their dependence on the intermediaries for information as well as distribution. E-Choupal, however does not attempt to completely eliminate the intermediaries as intermediaries can also add value to the goods at different stages of the agricultural value chain. In the e-

Choupal model, intermediaries are used for storage, physical delivery to the processor and quality assessment. With this modification of the distribution channel of agricultural products, a company like ITC gets an opportunity to directly procure from the farmers, thus reducing the price at which they procure the agricultural commodities used as raw material for their food business. The farmers also get a better value for their produce.

ITC has established a total of 6,500 e-Choupals covering 40,000 villages across India. These e-Choupals cater to 4 million farmers spread in ten states of the country. (Source: http://www.itcportal.com/sustainability/embedding-sustainability-in-business.aspx). Using this model, the company is able to reduce its cost of production (by lowering down the cost of procurement) and consequently pass on the price benefit to the consumer, thus becoming more cost effective and competitive in the market. Moreover it is able to expand its reach and strengthen its presence in the rural markets. The rural farmers who owe their increased purchasing power and living standard to ITC e-Choupal readily buy the products offered by the company. With a meaningful contribution to the rural economy, e-Choupal qualifies to be a unique and exceptional business model driven semi radical innovation.

(3) HUL Project Shakti: 'Project Shakti' is a widely known initiative of HUL in the Indian rural market. The distribution channel of HUL is considered to be its major strength.However, establishing a robust distribution channel in the Indian hinterlands was a gargantuan challenge for the company owing to the widely scattered nature of the rural population.The business potential of a village would not justify the cost of establishing a full fledged distribution channel there. Notwithstanding the hurdle,the company wanted to penetrate in to the rural market.The company started approaching the women folk in the villages who are not working but had the potential to work and the willingness to contribute to the family income.The company would approach the self help group in the villages and would select a member from the self help group as a 'Shakti Entrepreneur'.These 'Shakti Entrepreneurs' are also called 'Shakti Amma'.These women are trained by the company to stock and sell products of HUL.These micro entrepreneurs so created with the HUL initiative,distribute the products of the company in villages and are thus able to contribute to their family income and improve the living standards of their families.These model enable HUL to expand its distribution and reach even to small villages while simultaneously empowering the rural women and giving them an opportunity to improve their living standard. By 2010,the company had tapped in about 45,000 women and trained them to become Shakti Entrepreneurs.Through these initiatives the company had extended its reach to more than 3 millon households in more than 1,00,000villages across India.

In the year 2010-11,the company launched another initiative 'Shaktimaan' under which the men folk in the 'Shakti families'were given a bicycle by the company using which they would travel to nearby villages and sell the products of HUL there.This would increase the sales revenues for the families and at the same time would increase the sales of HUL in rural areas.The company has developed more than 30,000 'Shaktimaans' across India.

It is an example of simple business model innovation through which the company is able to expand into the rural market without any substantial investment for developing the distribution channel.

(4) Hariyali Kisan Bazaar: Hariyali Kisan Bazar is a rural marketing initiative by DSCL (DCM Sri Ram Consolidated Ltd.).It is not simply a supermarket but a rural supermarket that specialises in selling agricultural products and meeting the occupational needs of the farmers.It is the largest chain of rural supermarkets in India.Each Hryali Kisan Bazar caters to an area of 20 km around the supermarket serving an average of 15000 rural consumers. A typical outlet caters to around 50,000-70,000 acres of agricultural land.

The farmers have been known to conventionally purchase their daily needs items and some basic agricultural inputs from the village haats.For other agricultural implements,tools and some shopping goods they visit the nearest towns and cities.The additional cost for the farmers for all such purchases include the cost of transportation,time and inconvenience.DSCL was able to spot a market gap here.While others were apprehensive about the scope of an organised retail chain for villages, DSCL saw an opportunity. By providing solution to all the broader needs of the farmers, under one roof, Haryali Kisan Bazar has created a unique value proposition. This meaningful value proposition has the ability to generate substantial business potential. It promises good profits for the company in a less explored market while simultaneously empowering the farmers and developing the neglected rural market.

Haryali Kisan Bazar qualifies as an innovation as it is a new way of selling the assortment of agricultural inputs to the farmers and is an unprecedented case of an organised retail chain and a supermarket catering exclusively to the rural consumer and the agriculturist. The essence of this innovation lies in the different value proposition provided to a different category of target customer. The target customer of Haryali Kisan Bazar is very different from that of any other supermarket of India and the value proposition has been carefully designed to cater to the specific needs of this target consumer. This simple innovation can rightly be called as a customer centric innovation.

(5) Portable ECG Machine from GE: The R&D center of GE at Bangalore developes products and product features keeping in mind the needs of the developing markets and the emerging markets. One of the healthcare products developed by it, the portable ECG machine, is an important contribution of the company to the rural health management. The machine is not only substantially low in price as compared to a full size ECG machine but also produces an ECG report at a negligible price. Moreover, it can be easily carried to those remote places where the doctors and the hospitals cannot afford a full size ECG machine. GE has been successful in developing a new product which is radically different from all the other advanced and bigger ECG machine. The innovation involves a radical change in the product design and product technology. This innovation qualifies as a technology driven semi radical innovation.

(6) **Maruti Real Value:** The living standard in the villages has seen a rapid improvement in the last decade. Along with this improvement the product purchase list of a rural consumer has also shown a significant change. Many consumers have graduated from bicycles to motor driven two wheelers. The demand of four wheelers have also surged in the rural market. Many consumers who cannot afford a new car buy a pre-owned car. Many such pre-owned cars purchased in the rural market and even in urban market come from the stable of Maruti. Maruti Suzuki saw a business potential in this

segment. Sensing this scope, the company jumped into the business of pre-owned cars with Maruti Real Value.

The company assesses the value of the old cars for the interested sellers and buys from them thus saving their hassle for scouting for a buyer. The company then repairs and overhauls these second hand cars and sells them to the interested buyers at a reasonable price. So while buying from an organised seller and a reputed brand name, the buyer is assured of a reliable product and a good deal. Before the launch of this business, the company earned from its car only once, ie, when it was sold as a new car to the customer. This business gives an opportunity to increase its earnings from a given car. The additional earning comes to Maruti when the car is sold as a pre-owned car in the second hand car market. Moreover, besides getting an opportunity to sell a new car to a seller of old car by luring him with some exchange propositions, the company also gets an opportunity to come in touch with a new set of consumers (the buyers of old cars) . When this new set of consumers further go up the social ladder, there is a fair chance that the company can sell new cars to them. Thus the company increases the life time value of its customers. This innovation was a business model innovation which has now been emulated by a number of other companies in the Indian market.

It is worth noting that though this innovation was initially conceptualised for the rural market, the business has paid rich dividends in the urban market as well.

(7) Arvind Mills Ruf & Tuf: An innovation that introduced jeans to rural India came from Arvind Mills. Jeans, for long, had been in fashion in the urban market but this fashion had not been able to trickle down the rural market. The reason was two fold. Firstly, the price of most jeans brand was beyond what would be afforded by the rural consumers who was used to wear tailor made trousers. Secondly, being habitual of wearing trousers stitched by the neighbourhood tailor, the rural youth was psychologically ill at ease wearing readymade jeans. Thus despite being some sort of aspirational product for the rural youth, no jeans brand had been able to penetrate into the rural market.

Arvind Mills   was able to overcome this barrier with an innovative offering, the Ruf & Tuf brand of jeans. This offering was able to bridge the gap between the rural youth's desire for fashion and his inconvenience of wearing a readymade garment as well as the inability to pay a high price for a piece of garment. Instead of offering a readymade jeans, Arvind Mills introduced a 'Ready to be stitched' Jeans for the rural consumer. The product package consisted of an unstitched denim cloth, rivets, chain and the 'Ruf & Tuf' label. The company made the product available at the village tailors and offered them a commission on the sales of the product. These tailors would convince the rural youth to buy the jeans and would stitch it for them. Thus for the village youth it would be an affordable, tailor made, branded jeans. It was this incremental innovation in value proposition and value network that opened up the rural market for the branded apparel for the first time.

(8) Shampoo Sachet: There was a time when shampoo was used in India only by the urban consumer and that too the consumer belonging to the middle income group , the upper middle class and the higher income group. At that time shampoo was available only in big bottles and was unaffordable by the majority of the masses. An initiative by CavinKare changed it all and made the country a major consumer of shampoo. CavinKare introduced a brand of shampoo called Velvette and later on Chich which was made available in sachets of 50 paise and 1 rupee. The sachet would contain shampoo sufficient for one time use. The representatives of the company would go to the villages and rural areas where many people had never used shampoo in their life and demonstrate the use of the product to the people. The representatives would gather a crowd around the promotion van and profess the virtues of the product. They would pull a small boy from the crowd and wash his hair with the product. The gathered people would then be asked to smell and feel the hair. This experiment soon made the rural folk familiar with the virtues of the product. Even urban consumers who were familiar with shampoo but abstained from its use because of the restrictive price of the big bottles started using shampoo extensively in this new form which was much affordable. This innovation in product form was soon emulated by HLL (now HUL) and later by all shampoo manufacturing companies doing business in India. All these companies now sell a huge volume of shampoo in the urban as well as the rural market. Shampoo sachets are more popular than shampoo bottles in the rural markets and small towns and cities of India even today.

(9) Jaipur Rugs: Jaipur Rugs is a handmade carpet manufacturing company headquartered in Jaipur. It has its manufacturing operations spread across villages in ten states of India. The carpets manufactured by the company are sold in more than forty countries across the world. The unique thing about the company is that all its looms and manufacturing units are located in the villages. The company has an independent weaver base of 40,000 artisans most of whom were unskilled labour picked from the villages and trained by the company to become skilled artisans. These people work in the looms installed by the company in their villages or close to their place of dwelling. The weavers receive an average incremental income of Rs. 3,000 per month. The company has a turnover of more than $14 million. Jaipur Rugs offers a good example of inclusive growth and is an acclaimed success story at the 'Bottom of the Pyramid'.

An initiative of the Jaipur Rugs Company is the Jaipur Rugs Foundation which is a non profit organisation. The organisation is involved in several activities including health care, education and training of the village folk in areas where Jaipur Rugs Company operates. The company provides skill development training and skill upgradation training to the villagers. Through its programmes, the organisation trains the unskilled villagers in the art of carpet weaving and teaches them the use of the latest techniques and tools for manufacturing carpets that meet the global standards. These newly skilled artisans then start working for the company. In this way the simple producers in the Indian villages are connected to sophisticated buyers across the world.

This business model brings in profits for the company while facilitating rural development.

****

CHAPTER 4

VALUE INNOVATION AND ARCHITECTURAL INNOVATION: THEIR RELATION AND SIGNIFICANCE IN RURAL MARKETS

A substantial proportion of the global population resides in the underdeveloped and underprivileged pockets of the world. A major chunk of this population consists of the poor and economically backward section of the society (which C.K. Prahlad calls the 'Bottom of the Pyramid'). Though this segment constitutes a significant percentage of the population, these people had been blatantly neglected in the past by the corporate entities and the marketers. This is a segment that has not been completely exposed to the wonders of the communication technology which has been a driving force in the rapid development and global unification of the market. The reward of modernization has discriminately eluded this section. The rural market in the developing countries including India forms an important part of this segment. Though it would be absolutely unjust to consider the entire rural population as the bottom of the pyramid, in the light of the findings of NCAER which shows that 'there are as many middle income and above households in the rural areas as there are in the urban areas', the fact that a major part of this market is economically weak as compared to their urban counterparts cannot be denied. This is a market which despite having an immense potential, has been widely neglected by most of the corporate players.

The urban customers having been exposed to the marvels of the modern technology have evolved and have reached a higher level of development which has taken the market to a higher degree of sophistication that has shaped their choice and preference of goods, services and technology. The rural market on the other hand, having suffered due to the lack of sufficient exposure to the developmental process, remains at a lower rung in the process of development and sophistication. Thus it would not be wrong to consider this market similar to the primitive urban market. On the strength of the same logic it would be a big folly to shun this market which is at a nascent stage of development. A proper business and marketing strategy may make this market equally potent and lucrative, if not more than the urban market.

However just as the primitive urban market required some breakthrough innovation to fast pace the event of development, this market also calls for some properly chalked out, relevant and path breaking innovations. Being on a different plane of market evolution, the taste, preferences, wants and likings of the Indian rural market are markedly different from those of the Indian urban market. Hence, as discussed earlier, making a foray into this market with the same products and strategies that are used to serve the urban market would be a strategic blunder for any organization. An innovation for the rural market should therefore focus on certain important factors like the specific need of the rural customers, the purchasing power of the rural market, the consumption pattern of the rural folk, empowerment of the rural customer and the enhancement of their production capacity/potential. The innovations should essentially be comfortable on the pockets of the rural customers, be development friendly for the rural masses and give them an opportunity of growth, employment and enhancement of their living standards.

The call of the hour is to ponder upon the different dimensions of innovation for effectively penetrating into the rural market, and to identify a pattern of innovation that would both enhance the fortune for the bottom of the pyramid and would be effectively rewarding for a company working at the bottom of the pyramid. It is also imperative for organizations and researchers alike to make an attempt to understand the dynamics of the relationship between the types of innovation, organizational growth prospect (fortune at the bottom of the pyramid) and rural development through the development of the rural consumers and rural producers (fortune for the bottom of the pyramid).

WHAT THE RESEARCHERS SAY

The market dynamics are changing fast. New markets are emerging rapidly and are becoming attractive destinations for marketers. These markets open up a plethora of possibilities of experimentation and opportunities to move away from the convention. The real market promise in the future is expected to come not from the developed markets and the sophisticated market segments but from the underprivileged segments and the tier IV markets across the world which though largely untapped till now, have the potential of exhibiting a substantial rate of growth if catered to properly. "Managers who focus on gross margins will miss the opportunity at the bottom of the pyramid; managers who innovate and focus on economic profit will be rewarded". (Prahlad et al., 2002).

However catering to these lesser tapped markets including the rural markets call for a radical restructuring of the business process and developing marketing approaches to suit the demographics and psychographics of the newly discovered markets. While the MNCs aspire to capture a substantial market segment in emerging markets their marketing strategies are ill adapted to cater to the consumers in the market.

"The result is low market penetration, disappointing market shares and poor profitability". Thus an effective penetration into the emerging markets call for a rethinking of the marketing programmes directed at these markets. (Davar et al., 2002). Such an exigency directly point to the essentiality of innovation in business systems, business processes and marketing programmes. Innovations targeted at the BOP markets are less about discovering the new 'Who's' and much more about discovering a new value proposition (a new what) and a new value network (a new How) (Anderson et al., 2006).

As in the BOP market an effective penetration into the rural market also requires a judicious use of innovation. Innovation must be used in such a way so as to avoid undesirable inclusion or undesirable exclusion. In order to effectively survive in the rural market and to bring about a sustainable growth there, it is important that the neglected rural lot are treated not merely as consumers but are strengthened as producers (Jaiswal, 2008). Thus sustainable growth in the newly discovered rural markets requires the use of innovation not only to penetrate into these markets as sellers but also to ensure a simultaneous exploitation of the resources in these segments, develop business propositions around these resources and sell the resultant produce in the other markets. Such use of innovation to bring about a balanced growth in the rural markets and develop these markets

60

both as producers and consumers would also ensure survival for the practicing companies. Some entrepreneurs from these underprivileged markets have started evolving and moving towards the international markets riding on some sort of innovation. Study shows that Entrepreneurs from emerging economies are increasingly using innovation to enhance their customer support capabilities with the aim of efficiently serving their important international customers and penetrating the global markets in an effective way. (Khavul et al., 2010).

PENETRATING RURAL MARKETS THROUGH MARKET DRIVING INNOVATION

Today, in the midst of innumerable companies in the market with similar offerings and 'me-too' products vying for a substantial share of the consumer's pocket and many a times wooing the same set of consumers, the marketing game indeed is a gory battle and the market is an arena of cut throat competition. Darwin's theory of 'Survival of the fittest' aptly applies to companies and organizations that aspire to survive through this competition. Subtle and meaningful changes in the business process and some conspicuous mutations in the marketing thoughts may go a long way in enhancing the organizational fitness that would ensure sustainability and survival. Some notable areas of marketing function that call for a deliberate mutation are those of identification of market segments for penetration and the process of innovation adopted to facilitate penetration and to consolidate the market presence. It is imperative for companies to identify such markets that hold the promise for tomorrow and to effectively innovate to enter and survive in these markets. Out of several such markets, the rural market in the developing countries poses a strong candidature to qualify as a market with immense potential and 'fortune' for the marketer (Prahlad et al., 2002).

However the challenge for a business organization lies in understanding the specific need of this ostensibly dull market and providing the right products and right solutions through the right processes. In simpler words, innovation is the key for this market with an immense latent potential.

The pressing need for innovation would make an aspirant of the rural market ponder upon the types of innovation that would be most suitable for penetrating into the Indian rural market. With reference to the discussion in the last chapter it can be stated that when innovation has to be used as an instrument of rural market entry, business model innovation gets an edge over technology innovation. Once it is realized that for a company to penetrate into the Indian rural market, business model innovation is a smarter choice, one would like to explore the different types of alternatives within this category of innovation.

INNOVATIONS THAT MAKE SENSE

Speaking in Broad terms, business model innovation may be categorized into one of the two types: Innovation in Value Proposition and Innovation in Value Network (See Figure 1). While Value Proposition signifies 'What to Deliver?', Value Network as a term explains 'How to Deliver?'. Whether a company would go for innovation in value proposition or innovation in value network, depends on the competence of the company as well as on its strategy. Choosing between the two is a matter of strategic decision for the company. "Thus when Philips decides to enter the rural market, riding on the strength bestowed to it by its brand awareness, brand familiarity and brand acceptability it relies on its ability of product innovation and value innovation. Nonetheless, at the same time the company treads cautiously on the route of innovation leading to a new market when it decides to launch products as simple as battery driven lanterns and stoves as the initial offerings for the rural market. Unlike its radically innovative products like "light shower" and "light alarm" for the well heeled urban market where a definite result can be predicted through the use of such cutting edge technology, the products for the rural market are at the lower end of the value spectrum." (Chattopadhyay et al., 2010). The innovation it adapts for the rural market is by no means a radical innovation or even a discontinuous innovation in value proposition but an incremental innovation in its value proposition. This strategy for innovation, which falls short of a discontinuous value innovation, is like immersing a toe in a tub of hot water to judge its temperature, would give a feel of the market and prepare the base for further strategic innovations for the rural market. It might be an effective strategy to overcome the risk of loss and failures associated with value innovation and yet provide the competitive advantage that an innovation would provide in a market less explored.

In contrast to the huge investment and the risk of a substantial loss involved in the discontinuous innovation in value proposition, a discontinuous innovation in value network involves a much modest investment and a negligible risk of monetary loss in case of a failure. This type of innovation seems to be much more pragmatic for markets which are less explored and hence involve a greater degree of uncertainty. HUL'S entry into the rural market through 'Project Shakti' provides ample testimony to the fact. Hardly any real innovation was made in the nature of products for the rural market. The real innovation was in its design of the distribution channel wherein rural women seeking some gainful employment were roped in as distributors of the company which gave the company a three pronged benefit of being able to serve the social cause, reduce the cost of establishing the distribution channel and provide a momentum to its penetration strategy. The second category of innovation, besides being risk averse may seem to be much more lucrative for small organizations and new entrepreneurs who might find the extensive investment in R&D for Value Innovation beyond their means and resources.

Continuous Improvement in Value Network May Lead to a Unique Value Proposition

It is interesting to note that an incremental innovation in value network may accumulate over time to create a business model which offers a Unique Value Proposition. In other words a continuous and a well chalked out innovation in the Value Network may result in an innovative value proposition in the long run, at a much reduced risk of loss and a much lower investment. A case in point is Suguna Poultry. The business started as a small shop in a nondescript town of Tamil Nadu. Today it is a major player in India's Rs. 40,000 Crore poultry industry, thanks to its innovative value network. The company has spread its operations in ten states across the country and has aided the formation and development of fifteen thousand entrepreneurs who form an integral part of its supply chain and distribution channel. The company expanded its operations by primarily strengthening its supply chain system. Instead of investing in developing the infrastructure for establishing poultry farms, across the nation, the company approached the small and marginal farm owners at the local level for rearing the birds and taking care of the livestock at a stipulated fee. The farmers readily participated in the business process as it reduced their risk and ensured a steady income and regular earning. The company benefited by minimizing the capital investment and the cost of expansion and by achieving a rapid penetration and growth. This radical innovation in business model or business process created a win-win situation for the farmer and the company and propelled the growth of the business. This model has enabled the company to keep its total investment till July 2008 to about Rs. 1,000 Crore. (The company started using this model of operation from the year 1992.).

Having managed to save an enormous amount of money on investment, Suguna soon embarked on backward integration. Thus this model of business helped the company establish a hatchery to supply day old chicks to the contract farmers, to establish a 'parent farm' for rearing the parent breed and to set up a network to directly procure maize and soya which are key poultry feeds. Thus the incremental innovation in value network enabled the company to expand the business through backward integration. Moreover it provided the company with the strength, confidence and the resources required to diversify the business, develop value added products and go for value innovation as is evident from the company's foray into branded eggs- an innovation in value proposition- targeted towards health conscious people, and ready to cook and ready to eat packaged chicken products. The story of Suguna is the story of a Company's growth propelled by innovation. It is also a story of evolution from innovation in value network to innovation in value proposition. Thus Suguna is an apt example of radically innovative value network giving rise to a radical innovation in value proposition, which in turn makes the company a Market Driving Company in the real sense.

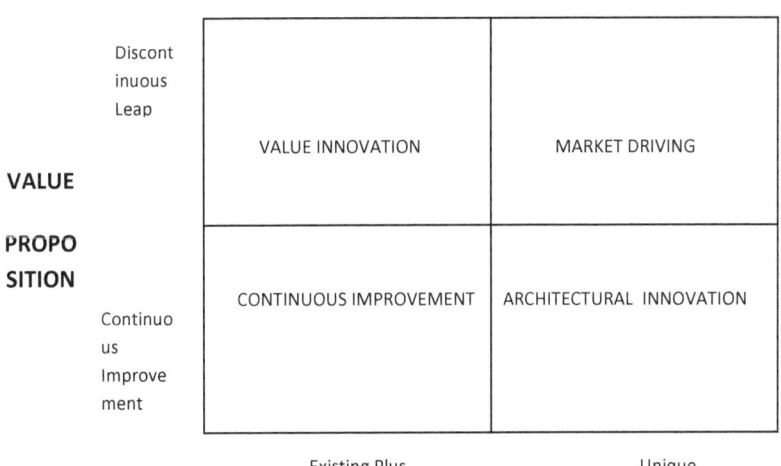

Figure 1: STRATEGIC INNOVATION

Source: "Marketing as Strategy", Nirmalya Kumar

INNOVATIONS TO STRENGTHEN THE RURAL PRODUCERS AND THE RURAL CONSUMERS

The Suguna model of business also brings to light another fact related to the development of the rural market or serving the 'Bottom of the Pyramid'. The bottom of the pyramid can be served best by treating the market not only as potential customers but also by developing the production potential at the bottom of the pyramid and if possible integrating the customer into the production process or the supply chain of the business. Suguna's growth would never have been so exemplary had it not tied up with the contract farmers and developed them as its supply chain. Success of Suguna also means the success of thousands of marginal farmers in the poultry business and their success in turn means the success of Suguna. This is a mutually beneficial relationship which creates a sense of belongingness amongst the farmers in the supply chain and synergises the entire business operations of the company. The synergy attained through this integration brought about by process innovation expedites the growth of the company and provides a significant competitive advantage. A model of business developed on the strength of such integration remains fairly preemptive.

Evaluating this model with the help of Michael Porter's five forces model we find that the business would be able to develop a market which would be attractive by virtue of each of the five forces being in favour of the business:

Segment Rivalry: Looking at the segment rivalry from the company's point of view we find that the innovative way of doing business, particularly the innovation in value networks, gives the much required cost advantage for operating in the rural market and provides a competitive advantage over the other players. Being able to develop as a market driving company will establish the credentials of the company as a market leader and diminish the adverse impact of segment rivalry.

Bargaining Power of Suppliers: Integrating the suppliers into the value chain of the business and making them a permanent and integral part of the business process would immensely reduce the bargaining power of the suppliers.

Bargaining Power of Buyers: Providing products at a lower price through innovative value networks and providing value addition through innovative value proposition strengthens the perceptual position of the product in the minds of the customers, enhances their preference of the company's products and loyalty towards its brand and thus virtually eliminates their bargaining power.

Threat from New Entrants: Establishing a strong value network and providing a Unique Value Proposition raises the entry barriers for non serious players, 'fly by night' operators and counterfeiters. Thus an overall impact of enhanced distribution, lower cost, improved value and partnership with the customer is a reduced threat from casual players and new entrants.

Threat from substitutes: An improved product at fair price which is easily available and offers value for money tremendously cuts down the threat of substitute products as well.

Another example that provides a good insight into the integration of the rural producer into the corporate production is that of the supply chain and production process of McFries. The Gujrati farmers from the Kheda district were motivated to grow a special potato 'Shepody potato' ideal for McFries brand of potato fries. The farmers were not only encouraged to supply the potato to the company but were also trained and given all the necessary technical knowledge for growing this variety of potato which can be upto a foot long in size. Till 2007, 90% of the potato used by McFries was imported. The company had been making an effort to develop and fine tune the technology to grow this special variety of potato on the Indian soil since 1997. Nine years of relentless effort paid off when the company was able to find a way to cultivate this special type of potato in two phases: The first phase consists of growing the potato for a few months in the colder regions of Himachal Pradesh to protect it from heat shock. The crop is harvested in the month of September and taken to the fields of Kheda district in Gujrat. In the second phase the tubers are replanted here to enable them to attain their proper size and maturity. The crop is finally harvested in February when it has grown fleshy and attained a size of upto 1 foot. The potato grown in this seemingly difficult way is much fleshier, with less water content, having a proper oblong shape and much larger and longer as compared to the conventional Indian variety of potato which is not ideally suited for fries. Drip irrigation employed for growing this variety requires much lesser amount of water as well. Thus potato grown in this way has a greater yield and fetches a much higher return for the farmer. No wonder then that the area under cultivation for the Shepody potato increased from a meager 7 hectares in 2005 to 1500 hectare in 2008. Sourcing the potato from the Indian fields saves McCain the cost of import. This innovative method of introducing an exotic variety in India and the innovative method of cultivation yielded results in 2008 when 70% of the potato used for making McFries by McCann India, was sourced from the Indian fields. Integrating the agricultural producer at the bottom of the pyramid with industrial production in this way not only increases the earning potential of the neglected lot but also enhances their exposure to modern means of production, and value added products and brands and makes them vibrant customers and a lucrative market for all sorts of products. The 'Bottom of Pyramid' thus calls for a more holistic approach whereby this impoverished and underprivileged lot, which forms the chunk of a developing country like India, should be treated not only as consumers but also as producers with a substantial potential. The key to tapping the market at the bottom of the pyramid thus lies in developing and upgrading the production potential and production capacity of this market.

Making Rural Producers/Entrepreneurs Partners in Architectural Innovation

The discussion above guides our thought to another aspect of innovation for the rural markets, i.e. innovation for the rural producers. Going by simple logic, when we are talking of architectural innovation, i.e. innovation in delivering the value, for the rural markets, architectural innovation for the rural producers forms one of the most important things to be pondered upon, more so in this era of globalization when the rural market cannot thrive in isolation.

Rural markets are in fact suppliers of a number of goods and services meant to be consumed by the urban markets and the international markets. Improvement in the quality of produce from these markets would improve their worth as producers and empower them as purchasers of various goods and services enabling them to join the global economy with a momentous force. Thus a well directed growth in rural production calls for some meaningful innovation. Green Revolution and White Revolution in India are perhaps the best examples of such architectural innovations which brought about an exponential growth in the productivity of the rural farmers and more importantly seamlessly integrated the rural producers with the national and the global economy. A major quantum of evolutionary growth at the bottom of the pyramid in India can be attributed to the Green Revolution and the White Revolution. Such initiatives if taken by the corporate players may go a long way in establishing partnerships between the rural entrepreneurs/producers and the corporate houses which in turn would help in developing an appropriate mechanism for exploiting the fortune at the bottom of the pyramid and developing the fortune for the bottom of the pyramid.

AN ALTERNATIVE PATH TO VALUE INNOVATION

A company may want to enter into the rural market either because of saturation in the urban market or to expand its business by tapping an unexploited market with a significant potential. In either of these cases, the modes of operation in the rural market would be markedly different from that in the urban market. A significant challenge would also be to choose a business model that would be innovative, serving the specific need of the market, less resource intensive, cost effective and at the same time sustainable. This makes it necessary for the company to go for an innovation that should be able to bring in a substantial amount of differentiation into the product but at the same time be cost effective. The simplest type of innovation that would be cost effective but be able to bring in a minor differentiation would be an incremental innovation in Value Network. Several such incremental innovations accumulated over a period of time may substantially differentiate the product without the company incurring a heavy cost in R&D. Thus this accumulated incremental innovation may pave the way for Architectural innovation that would encompass a radical innovation in the process of delivery as well as the innovation in the supply chain and distribution channel of the company (Figure 2).

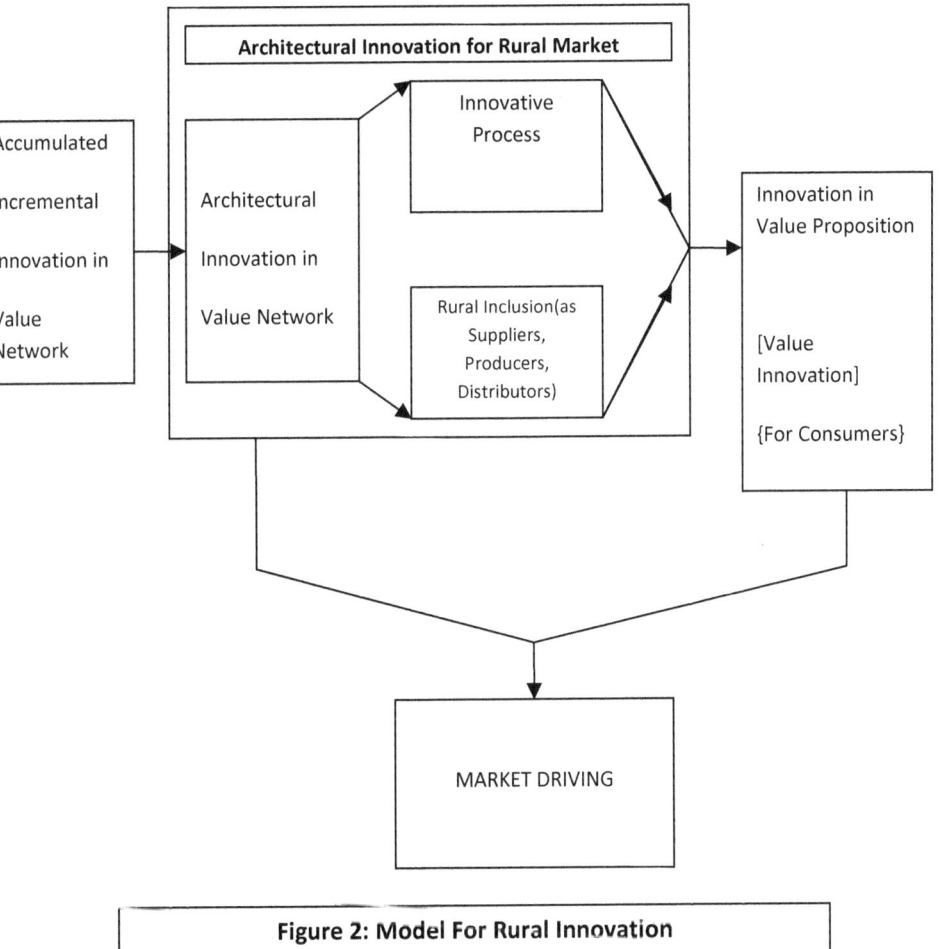

Figure 2: Model For Rural Innovation

Figure 2 depicts the relationship that can be inferred between the types of innovation, organizational growth prospect (fortune at the bottom of the pyramid) and rural development through the development of the rural consumers and rural producers (fortune for the bottom of the pyramid).

Source: Chattopadhyay et. al, "Market Driving Innovation for Rural Penetration",; The IUP Journal of Business Strategy, Vol. VIII, No. 3, 2011

This would be possible with a well chalked out plan for innovation for sustainable development. Architectural innovation has the potential of completely differentiating the company's offer from that of its competitor. Having grown with the support of architectural innovation, the company is now in a position to invest (the savings from its frugal operations) on value innovation and offer a superior value proposition to its customers. Having integrated its innovations (Architectural Innovation and Value Innovation) at this level the company glides on to become a market driver (See Figure 2).

For this gradual transformation from being a new entrant into the rural market to become a potent player at the bottom of the pyramid, the company's plan for innovation should focus on innovation at the following levels (See Figure 2):

1. Incremental innovations in the value network and the integration of several such incremental innovations in the initial phases.

2. Architectural innovation which encompass innovations in the delivery process and supply chain system.

3. Innovations for rural producers and their integration into the company's production system.

4. Value innovations for the customer.

Diligent planning and integration of innovation at these different levels may go a long in facilitating the company's penetration into the un-treaded terrains of the hinterland and in establishing the company as a market driver besides giving it the much required competitive advantage.

CHOICE OF INNOVATION AND FACTORS AFFECTING THE CHOICE

Clubbed between the two broad phenomenon of Value Innovation (Innovation in Value Proposition) and Architectural Innovation (Innovation in Value Network), which represent two distinct facets of business model innovation, lie hidden a plethora of issues representing the various hues of innovation. The decision regarding which aspect of innovation to bank upon to propel the value delivery system may depend on a myriad of factors like the nature and size of the firm, the type of product and services, the type of rural market segment targeted, the maturity of the chosen market, etc. Depending on the requirement, suitability and efficacy of the different types of innovations the firms might use the route of technological innovation in the products or services and their manufacturing or that of innovation in the way the products are delivered to the market i.e., modifications in the supply chain management, distribution channels or customer service networks.

Cost Innovation and Value Engineering: In rural markets where the consumers are very price sensitive the challenge for a manager lies in 'Cost Innovation' (which broadly refers to providing an enhanced value at the same cost or the same value at a reduced cost or in certain cases providing a slight compromise in value at extremely lower costs.) and 'Value Engineering'. Value Engineering refers to comparing any proposed change in cost with the likely change in customer value. The much talked about offerings from Tata in recent times such as 'Tata Nano' and 'Swatch', the water purifier for the economy segment, are good examples of cost innovation and value engineering that have opened up lucrative niche markets with substantial profit potential for the company. Thus steering successfully in the fast emerging rural markets of today is difficult in the absence of a comprehensive understanding of marketing innovations and their role in value creation and delivering value to the rural customers.

The present generation is witness to the fact that the rural markets are gradually yet steadily evolving and are on their way to become the hotbeds for future marketing activities. Also, a fact established beyond doubt is that these rural markets being different from their urban counterparts on several counts, call for a distinctively different entry mode, operations strategy and marketing strategy for an ensured success in these markets. This naturally presents a wide scope of innovation in processes, delivery and value proposition. The key to success lies in bringing in the required distinctiveness through innovations which are continuous, cost effective yet effective.

Some remarkable successes in the rural market bring to light the possibility of achieving architectural innovation through consistent and accumulated incremental innovation. Such architectural innovation can further be used as a platform for value innovation (a radical innovation in value proposition). A combination of architectural innovation and value innovation can further be used strategically by the company to emerge as a market driving company and a market leader in the rural market.

****

CHAPTER 5

RURAL INNOVATION: HOW AND FOR WHAT

Innovating simply for the purpose of being different is of no use. Innovation has to be meaningful. An innovation is worthwhile when it adds some value to the life of the people who use it or for whom it is meant. A sort of prerequisite for innovation targeted at the Indian rural market is that it should make the life of the rural folks convenient and should in no way burden the rural people with the cost of innovation. For an innovation to be meaningful and valued for the rural market, it should focus on and contribute to the following areas:

- ➢ Reduction of Cost
- ➢ Enhance the standard of living
- ➢ Enable the villagers to emulate (Facilitate the Trickle Down Phenomenon)
- ➢ Aid Production
- ➢ Facilitate Connectivity

(1) **Reduction of Cost:** The average purchasing power of the people being low in many rural areas, the Indian rural market is by and

large price sensitive. Thus for the rural markets price does matter and to effectively sell in the rural market, price of the product or service is an important thing to be considered. Ability to reduce the cost of the product therefore makes a firm competent and competitive in the rural market. So when it comes to the rural market, an innovation that contributes to cost reduction receives a favourable response and a warm applaud.

Also an innovation that reduces the cost of operation and the cost of transaction for the rural producer is well received in the rural markets. The popularity of 'Jugaad', a makeshift motor driven trolley, can be attributed to both of these reaons. 'Jugaad' is a motor driven vehicle, a trolley (much like a tractor in appearance) which despite not being approved as a vehicle by the Automotive Research Association of India (ARAI) or the International Centre for Automotive Technology (ICAT), commonly plies on the Indian village roads. It is a crude vehicle made locally in the villages by using scrap from older vehicles and fitting a generator machine or a water pump that serves as the motor of the vehicle. Despite being an unauthorised and illegal vehicle it is much popular in the rural areas as it can be assembled and sold at abysmally low price and offers a cheap mode of transportation for men and material. The cost of transportation becomes substantially less when 'Jugaad' is used for transportation.

An interesting innovation that has been observed by the author is a 'Rs. 5' mobile shop. In places around Bareilly, a district town in western Uttar Pradesh, India, some entrepreneurs sell assortment of spices, pickles and sauce in packets of Rs. 5. The Rs. 5 assortments are loaded onto a cart fitted with a loudspeaker. The cart puller who doubles up as a salesman goes from one area to another announcing his arrival and assortment of wares. The entrepreneur achieves a twofold benefit in the process. Firstly he does not need to own a retail counter and saves the cost of maintaining a retail outlet. Secondly he is able to cater to a larger number of clientele spanning across a wide area.

(2) **Enhance the Standard of Living:** Innovations that directly or indirectly contribute to the standard of living of the rural people can be considered to be in the category of most important

innovation for the rural areas. Innovations in food availability and distribution, housing and shelter, healthcare administration and education directly contribute to the improvement of living standards. Innovations in communication technology, innovations that enhance accessibility to communication technology, innovations in transportation and mobility and innovations that improve the availability of consumer durables and non durables in rural areas, fall in the category of those innovations that indirectly contribute to the improvement in the living standards of the rural citizens.

The midday meal scheme launched by the Government of India for the school going rural children can be termed as a socially significant innovation that contributes to the social upliftment and well being of the villagers. Under the scheme the rural children are provided mid day meals in the village schools. The precondition for getting a meal is to attend the classes. In this way those poor and uneducated people who do not appreciate the relevance of education and would not have sent their wards to school, are lured to send their children to school. The innovative scheme has been designed to effectively deliver nutrition and basic education to the young generation rural Indians.

(3) Enable Villagers to Emulate (Facilitate the Trickle Down Phenomenon): Trends, fashion and developmental changes trickle down from developed countries to developing countries and within the developing countries these trickle down from the urban areas to the rural areas. Certain innovations expedite and speed up the process of percolation from the urban centres of development to the rural areas. Such innovations are meaningful as they enable the villagers to emulate the city dwellers and give them access to certain things which make life easier. These innovations facilitate the faster penetration of goods and services into the rural markets. Sachets and mini packs for shampoos, detergents, toothpastes and creams have done exactly the same thing. This simple innovation has been instrumental in making rural India relevant for FMCG business. From the viewpoint of rural consumers, the innovation is relevant as it has given them an opportunity to emulate the lifestyle of their urban counterparts and has made high quality products affordable for the rural people even at the bottom of the pyramid.

Similarly the innovation by Arvind Mills when they launched the denim brand 'Ruf & Tuf' allowed the rural youth to easily emulate the dressing style of the urban youth at an affordable price.

(4) **Aid Production:** An innovation may focus on improving the status of rural India as a producer. Innovators who aim at facilitating production and increasing rural productivity should essentially think in terms of appropriate technology instead of the latest technology. Thus in many rural areas where availability of electricity is a problem, implements should be designed to work using alternative sources of energy or should be battery driven. In order to cater to the requirement of small firms and factories, a stripped down version of the conventional implements may be offered.

(5) **Facilitate Connectivity:** Information & Communication Technology has revolutionised the way people live, work and do business across the world. Information empowers. The

penetration of mobile telephony in rural India has already bridged the gap between the villages and the cities. The villages that used to be isolated from the rest of the country are now well connected to the cities because of the rapid development of the telecommunication network and the penetration of the mobile network. All such innovations that facilitate and enhance connectivity in the rural areas are contributing and would continue to contribute to rural development.

Unlike that in the developed countries, the mobile service providers while selling their services in the Indian market focus on the volume of use and the number of users instead of the 'Average Revenue per User'. This makes the call rates in the Indian market one of the lowest in the world making the services easily accessible to the masses in cities, towns and villages. More importantly, the availability of prepaid recharge coupons in denominations as low as Rs. 5 and Rs.10 is a unique endeavour which may be termed as frugal innovation as well as customer centric innovation that makes the services affordable and exponentially increases the usefulness of the services for the rural consumers.

To be able to provide cheap call rates to the consumers, the service providers share their resources and infrastructure like the telephone towers wherever possible thus reducing their fixed cost and cost of operation by several times.

Establishment of 'Kisan Call Centres' (Call Centres for Farmers) to provide agriculture related free information to the farmers over the phone is also an endeavour that empowers the farmers and helps them in increasing their productivity.

SOME FOCUS AREAS FOR INNOVATION

An interesting thing about rural development in India is the dichotomous state of development. The standard of living of the rural people has improved over the years. The reach of television in the rural areas is as good as that of in the urban areas. As far as the use and penetration of mobile telephony is concerned, rural India is fast catching up with its urban counterpart. On the other hand there are a number of areas and sectors where the situation is dismal. Literacy in rural areas is just 71% in contrast to that of 86% in urban areas. A study conducted by NSSO in

January- June 2014 also found that merely 4.5% of males and 2.2% of females in rural areas have completed their graduation. (http://economictimes.indiatimes.com/news/economy/indicators/l iteracy-rate-at-71-in-rural-india-86-in-urban-survey/articleshow/47886609.cms). Child mortality in rural India is one of the highest in the world (Upadhyay, et al., 2012). Female mortality at child birth is also high. Villagers do not have an easy access to hospitals and advanced healthcare facilities in most parts of India. Electricity has not yet reached many villages and remote rural areas. People have to go to the cities for good quality higher education.

Though some development is taking place in rural India, there are areas in which rural India is far behind its urban counterpart. Education, health, employment and infrastructure are some of those areas where huge gaps exist between urban and rural development. These are four primary issues to be taken up for the development of any region. Deficiencies in these areas imply incomplete development. Thus the cause of rural development calls for innovations in education, healthcare, infrastructure and innovations for employment generation.

Rural education implies formal education and informal education, child education and adult education. Thus the scope of innovation lies in the subject content and delivery mechanism of education as well as in the methodology of vocational and occupation related education. The potential innovators in this sector may be the Government, the education councils/boards, universities, colleges and NGOs working in the education and rural development sector.

Innovations in healthcare include innovative methods of treatment, innovations in the delivery mechanism of the treatment, pharmacological innovations and innovations in medical equipments and instruments. Healthcare innovations may also encompass innovations related to women's health, child health, critical care patients, accident and trauma victims and innovations that contribute to low cost healthcare. Important contributors to healthcare innovations may be the Government, State Health Department, hospitals, medical research institutes,

Research & Development organisations, medical practitioners working in the field, pharmaceutical companies, companies manufacturing medical equipments, companies in the healthcare sector and NGOs.

HOW TO INNOVATE

Is there any specific, predefined and structured method that guarantees a successful innovation or a breakthrough innovation? Perhaps there is no single method that can be followed to come out with an effective innovation. Very often inventions and innovations happen accidentally. A good example may be that of Tea Bags which developed by an American tea merchant, Thomas Sullivan, in the first decade of the twentieth century were initially made for the purpose of providing samples to the customers but were mistaken by the users as a new form of tea infusers (Source: https://www.tea.co.uk/the-history-of-the-tea-bag). In contrast to purely accidental innovations, some innovations happen as a surprising outcome of a relentless effort in a certain direction (Example, Sidenafil [Viagra] for erectile dysfunction was an innovative product that was a by-product formed during the experiment conducted to develop some other drug). However there are a number of innovations, particularly the corporate backed/ corporate sponsored and government backed/government sponsored innovations that are diligently planned.

Though there is no fixed methodology for innovation, some organisations have been known to be the source of a number of innovations. They have differentiated themselves on the basis of their innovativeness and have proved to be much more innovative than many other organisations. For companies like Sony, Apple and Tata, innovation is an integral part of their organisational DNA. Even the most innovative companies of the world including the ones mentioned above do not adopt a fixed and rigid method for innovation. The thing that makes these companies more innovative than others is the organisational culture that is conducive to innovation. Such carefully crafted culture of innovation within an organisation promotes and nurtures innovation throughout the organisation. The culture of innovation encourages the people at all levels within the organisation to innovate and rewards them for their innovations.

The second thing that promotes innovation is an apt motivation for the innovators and the potential innovators. The Tata Innovation Forum has instated an award even for failed innovations. Sony also encourages its innovators to look for new uses for their innovations which failed to click. All innovative companies and organisations provide testimony to the fact that though there is no fixed method for innovation, there is a well tested mechanism that promotes innovation. An innovation conducive organisational culture and motivation and reward system for innovation form the essential ingredients of this well tested mechanism. Having said this, the question that calls for an answer is 'How to innovate for rural India'? In the light of the fact that innovation follows no specific method, but a certain ecosystem promotes innovation, the question can be reframed as 'Who can and who should provide an ecosystem for rural innovation?' Should it be the Government? Should it be the companies? Should it be some cooperative organisation or should it be some NGO? Maybe each of these entities has some role to play and perhaps none of them can create a substantial impact in isolation. All of these entities can together create the right ecosystem that would nurture rural innovation (which would include innovation for rural areas and innovation in or from rural areas) – the Government, through policy making; the companies, through their market penetration strategies and procurement strategies; the cooperative organisations, through their inclusive growth strategies and the NGOs through their social upliftment initiatives.

How to Innovate for the Rural Markets: Some Guidelines

Some broad steps worth being recommended for innovating for the rural areas as well as for innovating in the rural areas are:

1. Through Innovation Forums/ Competitions for Innovations (Example, Tata Innovation Forum, Henkel)
2. Through Spotting Indigenous Innovations
   a. Recognise the Jugaad Spirit
   b. Convert it to Commercially Viable Product
   c. Commercialise

3. Harnessing the Traditional Knowledge

4. Empathetic Thinking backed by Thorough R&D: Some innovations are so simple that all they require is empathetic thinking and thorough R&D.

****

CHAPTER 6

DISRUPTIVE INNOVATION FOR RURAL MARKETS

While innovations are required for the development of rural India, time consuming and cost intensive innovations do not fit the bill and seem overtly non pragmatic for the rural markets. The situation calls for small disruptions, explorative searches and low risk experimentation. Such disruptive innovations are cheaper, smaller, and simpler and can be indigenously developed. Intelligently conceived disruptions can expedite rural development and facilitate the creation of new markets.

CONCEPTUAL SHIFT FROM "THE FORTUNE AT THE BOTTOM OF THE PYRAMID" TO "THE FORTUNE FOR THE BOTTOM OF THE PYRAMID"

As pointed out earlier, it is important that the trade, industry and the government consider the rural India not merely as emerging consumer and potential markets but more essentially as indispensable producers of goods and services. An empowered producers and socio-economically uplifted villagers would eventually emerge as an evolved consumer who invariably would constitute a mature market. The need of the hour is to focus on the integrated development of rural India. This necessitates a paradigm shift and conceptual transformation from the highly revered phenomenon of 'Fortune at the bottom of pyramid to a more pragmatic and a wider concept of fortune for the bottom of pyramid.

DISRUPTIVE INNOVATION FOR CREATING "FORTUNE FOR THE BOTTOM OF THE PYRAMID"

A meaningful disruptive innovation comes with the chances of spreading across easily and of being adopted quickly. It may therefore contribute more effectively to the concept of 'Fortune for the bottom of the pyramid'. Disruptive innovation is all about discovering a simpler way or a simpler process of solving the existing problem using lesser resources and incurring substantially lower cost. Disruptive innovation may bring forth crude form of solutions and lesser sophisticated products or processes but the fact that really matters is that these types of innovation have the potential of disrupting the existing practice of doing things. Thus delivering more to more people through less resource is the forte of disruptive innovation. This virtue of disruptive innovation makes it an ideal candidate to be used as an instrument for the development of the masses at the bottom of pyramid in general and for rural development in particular.

C.K. Prahlad in his seminal work 'Forture of the bottom of pyramid' talks at length about exploring the opportunities that exists in the underprivileged sections of the world and exploiting them for commercial benefits by developing business propositions around these opportunities. The concept may serve some purpose for business organizations looking for new opportunities or avenues of growth and help them expand and penetrate into hitherto unexplored markets. The concept however appears dwarf in the context of bringing about a holistic and substantial development for the underprivileged sections like the rural sectors. It is about the time that a shift is made from exploring the fortune at the bottom of pyramid to creating a fortune for the bottom of pyramid (Refer Figure 2). To make sense in the context of rural development

Prahlad's theory thus needs to be appended to the concept of inclusive growth. The widely acclaimed model of 'e-chaupal' by ITC is precisely an example of this confluence. The ITC model serves as an excellent example of inclusive growth through disruptive innovation in its business process. The success of the cooperative structure of Amul can also be attributed to the same reason. Another lesser known yet an appropriate example is that of Jaipur Rugs. The company provides training facilities, market access and employment opportunities to the weaving communities across the country. The company helps the weavers in enhancing the quality of their produce, develops markets (domestic as well as international) for them and empowers them by proper utilization of their skills and channelization of their abilities. Selling these wares produced by the weavers after procurement from the rural areas generate substantial revenues to be shared between the company and the weavers. The business model developed around the inherent skills of the weaving community and the business proposition that thrives on the regular enhancement of these unique skills creates a win-win situation for the weavers as well as for the firm. Besides economic upliftment and social empowerment of the weavers, the firm also provides employment to hundreds of rural youth by training them as supervisors and quality control officers.

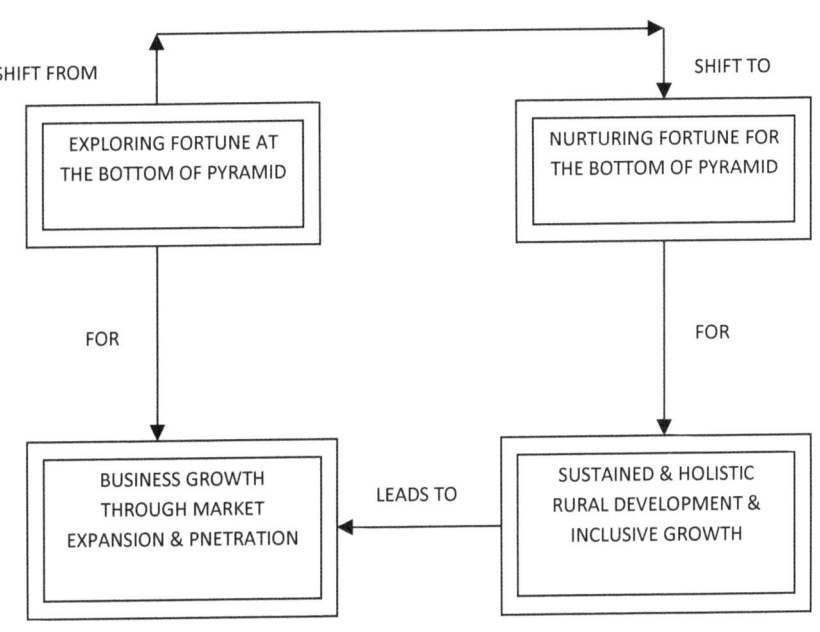

FIGURE 2: DESIRED SHIFT FROM THE CONCEPT OF 'EXPLORING THE FORTUNE AT THE BOTTOM OF PYRAMID' TO THAT OF 'CREATING FORTUNE FOR THE BOTTOM OF PYRAMID'

Another successful example of disruptive innovation and the one already discussed in the previous chapter is the innovative business model adopted by Suguna poultry to expand its business throughout the nation, by partnering with the small and marginal poultry farmers in the hinterland and integrating them into the supply chain of the company. The innovation is paying rich dividend to the company and ensures a sustained growth for the company as well as the smaller and underprivileged entrepreneurs at the rural level. The company provides day old chicks to the contract farmers and arranges for other inputs like feed, vaccination and health check-ups for these chicks on a regular basis. The farmers are encouraged to rear these birds for a stipulated fee. The full grown birds are procured by the company to be further processed or marketed. The company has spread this operations in ten states across the country and has created and developed fifteen thousand rural entrepreneurs who today form and integral part of the company's supply chain. The company has emerged as one of the major players in Rs. 40,000 crores poultry industry of the country.

When the objective is to enrich the life of the rural people and to simplify things for them, innovations need not always be a costly affair. The initiative taken by the research center of GE at Bangalore to launch a portable ECG machine that can be carried in a small bag, for the rural market has been able to influence the dynamics of the health care service in rural India. ECG reports that would otherwise require a patient to pay around Rs. 800/- can now be made available at around Rs. 25/-. The tremendous value of this innovation made it an ideal candidate for reverse innovation when the company introduced the same product into the US market as an essential instrument to be carried in ambulances and mobile dispensaries. The fact that makes such innovations relevant for the rural market is the immense benefit offered by the value proposition, their potential to change the long standing practices, their ability to radically change the life style and all these at an incredibly low cost of R&D and production.

A holistic rural development can thus be achieved through making innovation an integral part of a broad based plan for development. New ideas processes need to be introduced to hone the skills of the rural folk, enhance their productivity and to ensure the availability of advanced benefits and solutions and to facilitate a superior living standard for the rural folk.

****

CHAPTER 7

RURAL INNOVATION: SERVICE AT HEART

"You will find, as you look back upon your life, that the moments

when you really lived are the moments when you have done things

in the spirit of love."

— *Henry Drummond*

Before coming to the end of the discussion on "Innovation for Rural India", we would like to point out an interesting observation. There is a difference in the way the concept of "Innovation for Rural India" is looked at and approached by multinational companies and that by the small, nondescript innovators who strike upon a successful innovation and make it to the newspaper headlines after years of slogging in the hinterlands of India. While the former type finds mention in the Business Sections and Business Pages of Newspapers, the latter are widely acclaimed as selfless social service and rightly so. While one may argue that even the latter, ie, the 'non corporate innovations' or the 'social entrepreneur driven innovations' have tremendous business potential, the fact remains that the genesis, the DNA and the 'motives at the heart' of a corporate innovation are starkly different from those of a 'non corporate' or 'entrepreneur driven' innovation. The genesis and motive of a 'corporate driven' innovation is the desire to beat competition and to thrive. The motive here is also to milk profits from seemingly unattractive and hugely untapped markets. On the other hand, the genesis of a 'non corporate' innovation is the realization of and an empathy to the problems faced by the rural folks. The motive in this case is to develop some effective, easy and affordable solution for the 'not so privileged' masses.

Another difference can be spotted in the marketing approach adopted for the innovative products and in their acceptability. The innovative products born out of 'corporate driven' innovations are usually backed by a robust marketing support and huge advertising expenditures while those born out of non corporate innovations get promoted through word of mouth. Also in the former case customer adaptation of innovation requires a strong 'Push' approach to be adopted by the marketing team backing the innovation while in the latter case customer adaptation of innovation occurs somewhat spontaneously as a result of the 'Pull' phenomenon arising from the consumers' end and triggered by informal reference points or informal reference groups. Thus for an innovation to be truly successful in the rural market without any advertising support, it is important that the innovator understands the rural people, their woes, hardships, difficulties, problems and their way of leading their life. An innovation brought about in this way may not be a business driven innovation and yet have the potential of generating business.

1. **The Story of the Sanitary Napkin Man of India:** A story that proves the point mentioned above is the success story of Arunachalam Muruganatham, the sanitary napkin man of India.

   Muruganatham was astounded by the archaic methods of menstrual protection used by many rural Indian women. On probing he came to know that the reason for the use of outdated methods of menstrual protection was the high price of the sanitary napkins sold by the companies in the Indian market. These napkins were unaffordable for the poor women of rural India, who would be required to cut down on their milk budget to purchase these napkins. With this began the crusade of Arunachalam Muruganatham to develop a good quality sanitary napkin at an affordable price. After extensive research of the type of material being used by the multinational companies for making the pads and the technology used by them for the purpose, he came to the conclusion that the same quality of pads can be manufactured using much simpler technology. Muruganatham's persistent research and his quest to simplify a complex technology led to the invention of a low cost, inexpensive, small and simple machine for manufacturing sanitary napkins. Unlike the huge machines currently being used by the big manufacturers of sanitary napkins, Muruganatham's machine could be installed in small rooms and even in households for individual use. Manufacturing using this machine is so easy that it can be learnt even by a layman in less than half an hour.

The motive behind this superb invention was to increase the percentage of sanitary napkin users in rural India from 2% to

105

100%. Because of this life changing and women empowering invention and because of its impact on rural women of India the underprivileged women across the world, Time Magazine, in the year 2014, recognized Arunachalam Muruganatham as Time Magazine's 100 most influential people in the world.

2. **The Story of Tamul Plate Marketing Pvt. Ltd. (TPMPL):**

Like the above example, the story of Tamul Plate Marketing Pvt. Ltd., an entrepreneurial venture of Arindam Dasgupta, is also a success story that owes its origin to the motive of empowering the rural folks.

Arindam Dasgupta who hails from Assam, a state in the NorthEastern part of India realized that Assam is the largest producer of Betel Nut (Arecanut) in the country with at least 100,000 hectares of areca nut plantation. Though the betel nut is widely used in the region, the sheath attached to the areca nut leaf that covers the areca nut fruit is considered to be a waste. At the same time Dasgupta learnt that several firms in the southern part of India were using this sheath to manufacture disposable plates, saucers and bowls. He saw an opportunity to empower the villagers and betel nut growers by optimal utilization of a resource that was present in abundance but was considered to be a waste till that time.

Dasgupta started his work by creating awareness among the villagers regarding the profitable use of areca nut leaf sheaths and the possibility of earning money through it. He then encouraged the villagers to establish micro manufacturing units, for manufacturing areca nut leaf plates and dinnerware, at their plantations. The simple machines required for manufacturing these disposable dinnerware was sold to the manufacturing units by TPMPL with 100 percent buyback guarantee for the plates. Thus TPMPL started operating with a simple two tier business model. At the first level are the decentralized micro manufacturing units located at different plantations across the region. TPMPL collects the finished products from the village level producers. At stage 2, the company conducts centralized quality checking and packaging of the finished products and then markets them in several states of the country. This model of functioning provides the farmers with a unique business scope and provides them an opportunity to run a profitable business using raw material that is available to them free of cost. TPMPL also manages to keep its cost of production and procurement considerably low. It is a win-win situation for the poor farmers as well as for the company.

3. **The Story of EVOMO, the Rural Utility Vehicle:** Another innovation, albeit still in the confines of the lab, that owes its genesis to an altruistic spirit is the Rural Utility Vehicle, named as EVOMO (an acronym of Evolving Mobility) by its inventor, Abhinav Das.

A crude, makeshift and unlicensed multi-purpose vehicle often seen on the rural roads and commonly known a 'Jugaad' (which literally translates to makeshift) has adorned the Indian rural scenario for quite some time. Made from scrap, old automobile parts, wooden planks and electric motors used in water pumps, 'Jugaad' has been the poor man's multi-utility vehicle. However, because of its crude design and abysmally poor safety standards it does not have the required certification from Automotive Research Association of India (ARAI) or from the International Centre for Automotive Technology (ICAT) and hence is unsafe and illegal to drive.

Being aware of the specific needs of the villagers and their paying capacity for the ownership of a vehicle, Abhinav Das, a young entrepreneur and engineer designed a no frills vehicle much superior in structure, design and safety measures, yet comparable in price to 'Jugaad'. UNLIKE 'Jugaad', this rural utility vehicle named 'EVOMO' is made up of automotive components and offers better mileage, comfort, safety and aesthetics at more or less the same price. The vehicle is still in the designing and experimental phase and has not got the required certification and permission to ply on the road yet. Once it is ready to take to the roads, it has the potential to revolutionise and redefine mobility and to change the rural landscape.

4. **The Story of Glocal Healthcare Systems Pvt. Ltd.:** One of the best examples of innovation in healthcare management arising from a keen desire to serve the rural people, empathy for the suffering and the motive of providing affordable healthcare for the underprivileged is that of Glocal Healthcare Systems Pvt. Ltd.

The unique selling proposition of Glocal Healthcare is quality healthcare at very low cost. The most important instrument in designing this low cost, no frills model of healthcare is the realization of the fact that only 42 diseases account for 90% of the disease load in rural India and that 95% of the healthcare needs can be met with secondary healthcare. This knowledge served the basis of the low cost healthcare strategy at Glocal. The healthcare system was designed to effectively treat these 42 diseases.

The costly medical instruments and equipments which are commonly seen in all hospitals but are not essential for the treatment of these 42 ailments were not installed in the Glocal chain of hospitals. With the help of a carefully designed Hospital Management Information System, that has been diligently fed with data related to the symptoms, diagnosis, testing requirements, medication, drug interactions and contra-indications for the 42 identified diseases, the hospital has been able to standardize and expedite the treatment and patient care. The examining doctor feeds the personal data of the patient and data related to the symptoms experienced by him/her in a standardized online form and the Medical Diagnosis and Management System, which is a part of the Hospital Management Information System, provides the doctor with the necessary diagnostic and treatment assistance. This system has also helped to drastically reduce the time taken by OPD patients for their medical checkup, diagnostic tests and getting their reports from an average of 6 hours to 1.5 hours.

Systematic planning of instrumentation and installation of medical equipments at the hospital also helps to keep the costs low. Glocal does not purchase equipments from the regular vendors. Instead, the healthcare chain identifies the original equipment manufacturers, purchases components from them and gets the machines and equipments assembled by them in its hospitals. The treatment is further made affordable to the patient by selling good quality generic drugs instead of branded drugs in the pharmacies of the hospital. Cost of operations is also lowered down by having a centralized radiologist in the city of Lucknow. The X-rays done in all the hospitals of the chain are sent through email to the radiologist located at Lucknow. The reports for the X-rays done in the morning are sent to the respective hospitals by 2:00 PM and for those done in the afternoon and evening are sent by 8:00 PM.

Using this innovative model, Glocal Healthcare Pvt. Ltd. now runs five multispeciality hospitals, across the country, each with hundred beds. It is in the process of setting up fifty more multispeciality hospitals in the country. Fourteen of them are scheduled to be operational within the next twelve months.

****

REFERENCES:

- *Anderson Jaime & Markides Costas(2006); "Strategic innovation at the base of the economic pyramid"; Harvard Business Online; August 2006*
- *Behl Teejesh N.S.(2009);"Jeez, It's Cheese"; Business Today, May 3, 2009*
- *Bhandari Bhupesh(2009); "Let There be Light"; The Startegist; Thursday, April 28, 2009*
- *Bhandari Bhupesh, "Let There be Light", The Startegist, Thursday, April 28, 2009*
- *Chattopadhyay Subho & Chandra Garima Jaiswal(2010); "Delivering Value Through Innovative Marketing"; Marketing Mastermind; July 2010*
- *Chattopadhyay Subho & Sarkar A.K. (2011); "Market Driving Innovation for Rural Penetration"; The IUP Journal of Business Strategy, Vol. VIII, No. 3, September 2011*
- *Davar Niraj N. & Chattopadhyay Amitava(2002); "Rethinking marketing programs for emerging markets"; Long range planning; Vol 35, Issue 5, October 2002*
- *Jaiswal Anant Kumar(2008); "Fortune at the Bottom or the Middle of the Pyramid?"; Innovations; Vol. 3, Number 1, Winter 2008*
- *Jaiswal Anant Kumar, "Fortune at the Bottom or the Middle of the Pyramid?", Innovations, Vol. 3, Number 1, Winter 2008*
- *Khanna Tarun, "Nurturing Entrepreneurship in India's Villages", The McKinsey Quarterly, November 2008*
- *Khavul Susanna, Peterson Mark & Rasheed Abdul A.(2010); "Going global with innovations from emerging economies: Investment in customer support capabilities pays off"; Journal of International Marketing; Volume 18, Number 4, 2010*
- *Klaauw Bas van der, Wang Limin (2011); "Child mortality in rural India"; Journal of Population Economics; Volume 24, Issue 2, April 2011, pp 601-628*

- *Kumar Nirmalya(2004); "Marketing as Strategy"; Penguin Publishing House, New Delhi; 2004*
- *Lee Richard K (2008); "Where innovation creates Value"; The Strategist, Tuesday, January 28, 2010*
- *Madhavan N(2008); "Radically Different"; Business Today; July 27, 2008*

- *Madhavan N., "Radically Different", Business Today, July 27, 2008*

- *Mitra Kushan(2009); "From Field to Fries"; Business Today; April 5, 2009*

- *Permanente K., "Innovation on the Front Lines", Harvard Business Review South Asia, September 2010*
- *Prahalad C.K. & Hart Stuart L.(2002); " The Fortune at the Bottom of the Pyramid"; Strategy+Business; issue 26, 2002*
- *Prahalad C.K. and Hart Stuart L., " The Fortune at the Bottom of the Pyramid"*
- *Sengupta Snigdha(2008); "This Bird Means Business"; Outlook Business; August 9, 2008*
- *Upadhyay Ravi Prakash, Chinnakali Palanivel, Odukoya Oluwakemi, Yadav Kapil, Sinha Smita, Rizwan S. A., Daral Shailaja,Chellaiyan Vinoth G., & Silan Vijay (2012); "High Neonatal Mortality Rates in Rural India: What Options to Explore?"; ISRN Pediatrics; Volume 2012 (2012)*

ABOUT THE AUTHOR

Dr. Subho Chattopadhyay
Associate Professor
LBSIMT, Bareilly (India)

Dr. Subho Chattopadhyay is a UGC-Net qualified Management teacher and academician with interest in the areas of Marketing and Brand development. Before foraying into academics, he has worked as a Sales and Marketing professional with regional leadership responsibilities with the pharmaceutical industry. During his career as a management teacher, he has conducted MDPs and been a resource person for training programmes conducted for the Ministry of MSME, University teachers and entrepreneurs. During his academic career he has presented several research papers in national and international conferences. His published work includes research papers in national and international journals, articles in magazines and chapters in books. Some of his research papers have been listed in Econbiz, Proquest and EBSCO database. He is teaching in the areas of Marketing and International Business.

He holds a Doctorate in Business Administration and

besides his interest in the study of innovation, his research interests include the study of brands and brand development, positioning of brands, brand positioning strategies in FMCG and International Marketing.

www.ingramcontent.com/pod-product-compliance
Lightning Source LLC
Chambersburg PA
CBHW060349190526
45169CB00002B/533